OFF-ROADING VEHICLES

ATVs

TAMRA B. ORR

Mitchell Lane
PUBLISHERS

Parent and Caregiver Tips for Creating Nonfiction Readers

The high-interest topics in the *Off-Roading Vehicles* series are sure to get your young reader excited about reading nonfiction. While exploring a fascinating subject, your reader will be introduced to new concepts, facts, ideas, and vocabulary.

Tips for Reading Nonfiction

Talk about Nonfiction

Explain that nonfiction books provide facts about real-world topics. When readers read nonfiction, they gain a rich understanding of the world. They build background knowledge that provides a foundation for learning and academic success.

Look at the Parts

This book contains the following helpful features. Share the purpose of each feature with your reader.

Photos, Captions, and Graphic Aids

The photos, captions, charts, maps, and other graphic aids in nonfiction texts contain a wealth of information. Help your reader identify different ways information can be displayed. A special feature, "A Closer Look," puts the spotlight on learning through images.

Sidebars

These extra tidbits of information help satisfy readers' curiosity and expand their knowledge.

Table of Contents

Located at the front of the book, this list shows the big ideas within the text and the page numbers where they can be found.

Glossary

Located at the back of the book, the glossary defines key words and phrases that are related to the topic. These words and phrases can be found in the text in **bold** type.

Comprehension Questions (Fact Check)

Multiple-choice questions help readers self-check to make sure they understand what they read.

Index

Located at the back of the book, the index is an alphabetical list of topics and the page numbers where they can be found.

With a little help and guidance, your reader will be on their way to enjoying and learning from nonfiction books.

Mitchell Lane
PUBLISHERS

mitchelllanepub.com

2001 SW 31st Avenue
Hallandale, FL 33009

First Edition, 2026.
Author: Tamra B. Orr
Designer: Kathy Walsh
Editor: Tricia Hoffman

Series: Off-Roading Vehicles
Title: ATVs / by Tamra B. Orr

Hallandale, FL : Mitchell Lane Publishers, [2026]

Library bound ISBN: 979-8-89260-563-2
Paperback ISBN: 979-8-89260-593-9
eBook ISBN: 979-8-89260-574-8

Photo Credits
Adobe: background, miloje; Alamy: p9, Lifestyle Pictures; p13, Andre Jenny; p15, William Mullins; p16, Avpics; p17, Mike Pellinni; p19, Andrii Biletskyi; p21, Amelia Martin; p22, NurPhoto SRL; p25, Earl Walker; p26, Sergey Sitnikov; p27 & 29, Dennis MacDonald; Shutterstock: Cover & Title pg, Sergei Domashenko; p 5, muroPhotographer; p 6, sockagphoto; p7, Bob Pool; p10, Fotogrin, Anatolly Kosola pov; p12, Amelia Martin; p14, Vytautas Kielaitis, p23, K-FK; p25, HeyPhoto; p29, muroPhotographer; p7 & 28; Alexey Stiop; p24 & 29, HeyPhoto; p25 & 28, Anton Tolmachov; p25 & 28, Maciej Kopaniecki

Contents

Get Ready

Tie the laces on your boots.

Pull on your gloves.

Adjust your goggles.

Strap your helmet under your chin.

Ready to go? It's time to ride!

Hopping on an ATV is exciting and fun. You can feel the adventure just waiting for you around the next curve or over the next hill.

Having a great time when you ride is almost a sure thing, but wearing the right gear and knowing how to stay safe are essential. Let's go!

Climb On!

ATVs are all-**terrain** vehicles. They are made to drive over rocks, through mud, and across creeks. They have been around for years for both work and play!

ATVs are used by farmers, police, firefighters, and the **military**. Thanks to their ability to maneuver quickly, ATVs are also used on construction sites and with search and rescue teams.

PUT TO WORK

ATVs are used on farms and ranches for everything from herding livestock and checking fences, to carrying equipment and maintaining fields.

From the 1960s to Today

ATVs were first invented for Japanese farmers in the early 1960s. By 1969, ATVs were being made in the United States. Originally, they had three fat tires and were sold as **recreational** vehicles. They were fun—but they were also dangerous.

Three-wheeled ATVs were banned in 1988 because of how often drivers were injured when the vehicles tipped over. Companies quickly switched to making four-wheeled ATVs. It was not long before national ATV races began.

ATVs originally had only three tires—one in the front and two in the back.

ON THE BIG SCREEN

U.S. ATV sales were boosted by celebrities. James Bond rode one in the 1971 film *Diamonds are Forever*. And so did Dwayne Johnson's character in the movie *Baywatch* almost 50 years later.

Meet the "Quad"

While ATVs differ from one manufacturer to another, they all have four special airless tires designed to grip the roughest terrain. Those tires are why some people call ATVs quads.

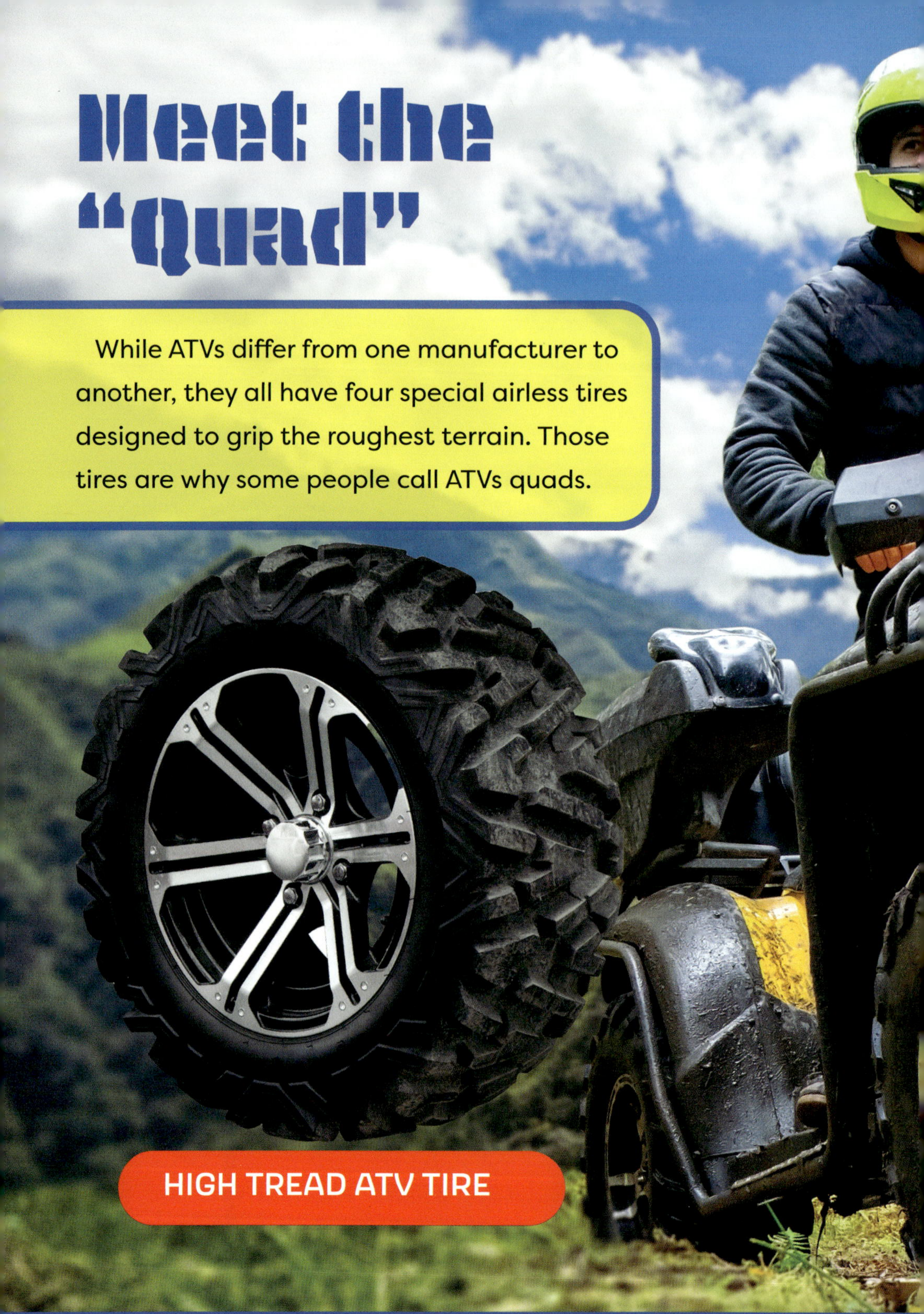

HIGH TREAD ATV TIRE

Almost all ATVs are designed for only one rider. ATVs' gasoline-powered engines are big and powerful. They often reach speeds of 65 miles (104 km) per hour. They have handlebars for steering. Some have front and rear brakes, while others have **linked brakes**.

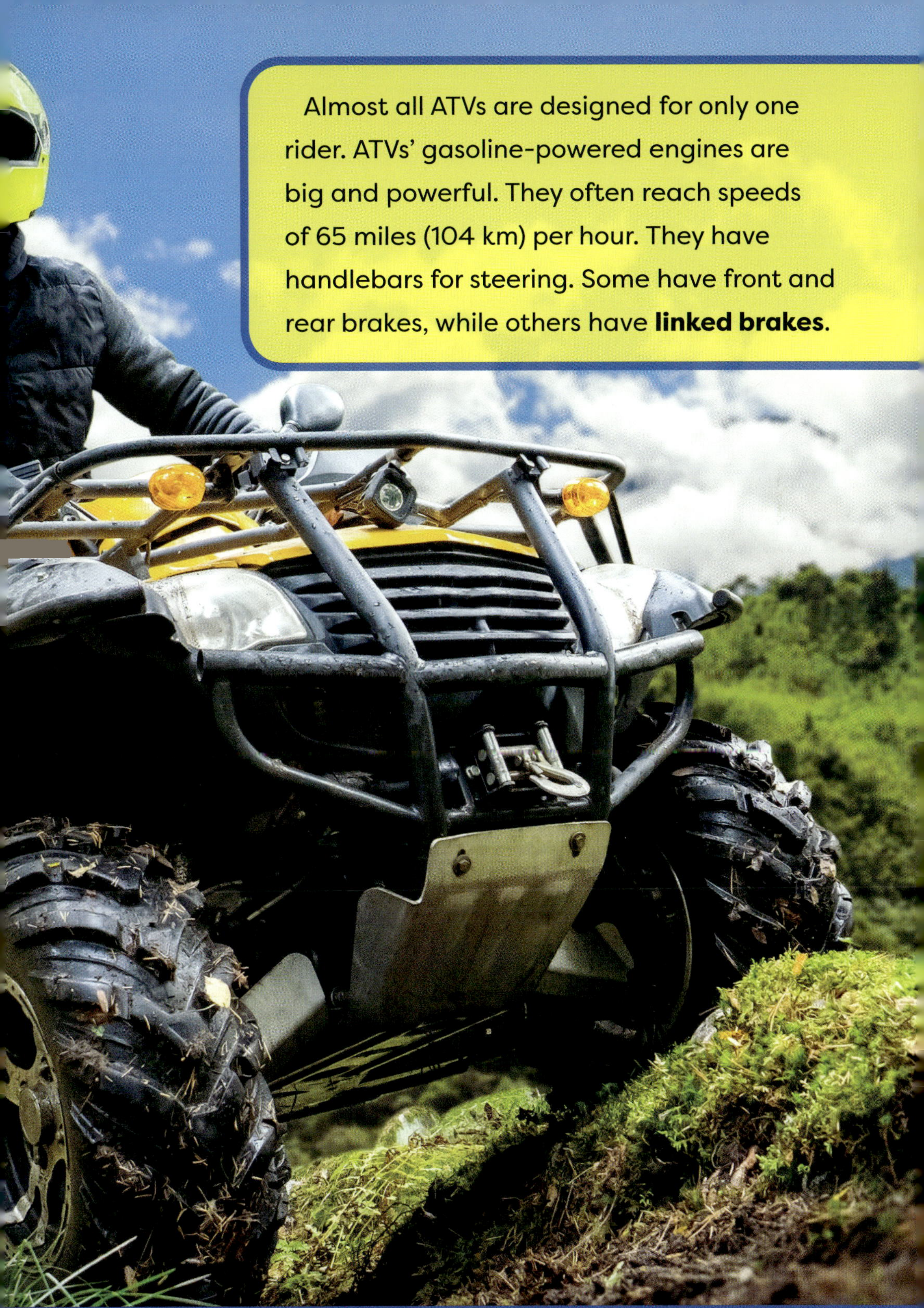

Youth ATVs are made for beginning riders. They have smaller engines, usually less than 70 cc (cubic centimeters). This is about the size of a lawn mower engine, so beginner ATVs have limited power. This keeps their speed down.

Unlike full-size ATVs, these models have either an automatic **transmission** or no gears at all. They are all two-wheel drive, so their power is sent to just the two rear wheels. They are specially designed to fit smaller hands and feet and shorter legs.

ALWAYS follow the manufacturer's minimum age recommendations. They are found on all ATVs' warning labels.

KEEPING IT LEGAL

There aren't any federal laws about the age at which a person can drive an ATV. Each state has its own guidelines. Be sure to check the rules where you live before hopping on!

Suit Up!

Riding an ATV safely starts long before you straddle the seat. It begins when you put on the right gear.

Helmets are very important. They protect your head from injury if you fall or hit something. **Shatter-resistant** goggles help keep your eyes safe from low-hanging branches or large bugs. The lenses should be tinted gray for sunny days or clear for night rides.

GET YOUR GEAR IN GEAR

All helmets should be safety-approved by the U.S. Department of Transportation, the American National Standards Institute, or the Snell Memorial Foundation.

Wearing wool gloves not only keeps riders' hands warm, but also protects them from rocks or branches. Boots with heels help secure riders' feet on the footrests. These boots should fit over the ankles.

Experts also recommend riders wear wool shirts under their coats, plus sturdy pants with kneepads. All clothing should be bright and colorful so that riders can easily be seen.

ARE YOU READY TO RIDE?

The American Academy of Pediatrics advises against kids younger than 16 driving or riding on an ATV.

Safety First

Along with wearing the right gear, you need to follow these important safety rules:

NEVER

- √ Take an ATV on regular streets. They are not made for paved surfaces.
- √ Add a second rider.
- √ Remove a hand from the handlebars.
- √ Drag your feet on the ground.

ALWAYS

- √ Tell someone before you ride, or only ride when an adult is with you.
- √ Follow your state's ATV laws.
- √ Read the manual for your ATV before riding.
- √ Check the weather before riding.

TIME TO STUDY

Before riding on an ATV, experts advise everyone to take an ATV safety course, like those offered by the ATV Safety Institute.

Straighten Up

Gear? Check!
Safety rules? Check!

Now it's time to focus on your **posture** when you ride.

When riding on an ATV, you must be able to shift your weight quickly and reach the controls easily. In order to do that, you should keep your:

- √ **head up**
- √ **eyes looking ahead**
- √ **shoulders relaxed with elbows slightly bent**
- √ **feet on the footrests with toes pointing straight ahead**
- √ **back straight**
- √ **knees in toward the gas tank**

PROCEED WITH CAUTION

Beginning ATV riders are 13 times more likely to have an accident than experienced drivers.

Tricks and Skills

Riding an ATV is fun—but learning special skills and tricks can be even better. DO NOT try to do any of them without an instructor!

The first skills to know are ones you will likely need on courses, such as handling hills and navigating around **obstacles**. After that, some possible tricks include cornering, or taking a turn very sharply, or popping a wheelie.

TIME TO PLAY

Want to "ride" an ATV, even when you're inside? Some video games provide virtual ATV fun. *ATV Offroad Fury* from PlayStation features dirt bikes, dune buggies, and ATVs.

Learn the Lingo

All sports and games come with their own **lingo**, and that is also true for ATV riding and racing. Learning the terms makes it more fun to talk to and understand other riders. Some of the most commonly used terms are:

- *Airtime:* the time a rider is in the air after a jump
- *Digger:* a crash or collision
- *Roost:* the dirt an ATV kicks up when the tires spin
- *Squid:* an unpredictable or reckless rider

AIRTIME

DIGGER

ROOST

SQUID

Hop On!

There is no question that riding ATVs is popular. According to the ATV Safety Institute, more than 35 million Americans ride these vehicles. Some do it as part of their work, but most ride ATVs for fun.

Many riders say there's nothing better than racing over rocks, plowing through mud, and traveling over wooded trails. Doing it safely is the first step. The second? Have fun!

TIME TO RACE

The Grand National Cross-Country race began using ATVs in 1980. The ATV National Motocross Championship series started in 1985.

A Closer Look

Why is this man riding his ATV around a herd of sheep?

ATVs are made for both work and play! They are often used on farms for jobs like inspecting crops, mowing grass, fertilizing crops, and herding livestock, like these sheep.

Why is this track so muddy?

Because it is part of the fun! ATVs are specially designed to push through deep mud, and races almost always include a muddy track just to add excitement to the competition.

Why did this ATV roll over?

Now and then, ATVs will roll over. This tends to happen when going around sharp turns or uneven surfaces. This rider knew to roll away from his vehicle. After making sure he is not injured, he will check to make sure his ATV wasn't damaged.

Is this ATV flying?

No! This rider is catching air by jumping on his ATV. After racing up a ramp, the vehicle and its rider soar into the sky. For a moment, it feels like flying!

Why is the man waving a flag?

A black and white checkered flag marks the end of a race. The first rider to get to it is the winner. Other colored flags are used in TV races, including several that warn racers if the track isn't safe for any reason.

Who says "eat my dust"?

A movie in the mid-1970s coined the slogan "Eat my dust." Today, it is sometimes said by ATV racers who are winning, because dust or mud from the course will fly in the faces of the riders behind them. This rider certainly has stirred up a dust cloud as he zooms to the finish line.

Glossary

lingo (LING-goh)

the slang terms used by a particular group of people

linked brakes (lingkt breyks)

a system that activates the brakes on both of a vehicle's wheels when one lever is pulled

military (MIL-i-ter-ee)

of or pertaining to soldiers or armed forces

obstacles (AHB-stuh-kuhlz)

something that gets in the way of movement or progress

posture (PAHS-chur)

the position of the body or its parts

recreational (rek-ree-AY-shuh-nuhl)

of or relating to recreation, fun, or relaxing activities

shatter-resistant (SHAT-ur ri-ZIS-tuhnt)

unbreakable

terrain (tuh-RAYN)

a section of land

transmission (trans-MISH-uhn)

a series of gears in a vehicle

Fact Check

1. ATVs have _____ for steering.
   A. tires B. footrests C. handlebars
2. The laws about the age requirements to ride an ATV change from _____ to _____.
   A. state to state B. year to year C. company to company
3. Youth ATVs tend to have ______ or no gears at all.
   A. airless tires B. automatic transmissions
   C. four-wheel drive
4. Cornering in an ATV means _____.
   A. taking a turn sharply B. shifting weight quickly
   C. dragging your feet

Answers: 1. C, 2. A, 3. B, 4. A

Further Reading

Amstutz, Lisa. *The Gearhead's Guide to ATVs.* Capstone Press, 2022.

Dickmann, Nancy. *ATVs (Wild about Wheels).* Pebble Publishing, 2020.

Hoena, Blake. A*TV Cheat.* Capstone Press, 2024.

Rogers, Marie. *ATVs* (*Let's Ride*). PowerKids Press, 2021.

On the Internet

ATV Safety Institute: ATV RiderCourse
atvsafety.org/atv-ridercourse/
Learn how to enroll in a 2-hour online e-course on how to safely ride ATVs.

ATV Safety Institute: Parents, Youngsters, and All-Terrain Vehicles
atvsafety.org/wp-content/uploads/2024/06/ASI-Parents-Youngsters-ATV-05-24.pdf
This detailed booklet covers how to determine your readiness to ride an ATV, as well as operating procedures and practices.

Nemours Children's Health: ATV Safety
kidshealth.org/en/teens/atv-safety.html
This site is geared toward teens who want to know the basics about ATVs, including safety guidelines and state rules.

Off-Road Vehicle Facts for Kids
kids.kiddle.co/Off-road_vehicle
Explains how off -road vehicles are used and includes lots of pictures.

Index

About the Author

Tamra B. Orr is a mom, wife, grandmother, and full-time writer and author living in the beautiful all-terrain Pacific Northwest. She is surrounded by more than 50 ATV riding trails in her state, with everything from dunes and desert to wooded trails and pathways. A graduate of Ball State University, she has written more than 750 nonfiction and educational books for readers of all ages and loves her job. It gives her the chance to learn about something new—and then share that information—every single day.